HANDBOOKS OF EUROPEAN NATIONAL DANCES

EDITED BY
VIOLET ALFORD

DANCES OF SCOTLAND

Plate 1 *A Reel*

DANCES of SCOTLAND

JEAN C. MILLIGAN
and
D. G. MacLENNAN

NOVERRE PRESS

ILLUSTRATED BY
ROWLAND A. BEARD
ASSISTANT EDITOR
YVONNE MOYSE

First published in 1950
This edition published in 2021 by
The Noverre Press
Southwold House
Isington Road
Binsted
Hampshire
GU34 4PH

ISBN 978-1-914311-1-32-1

© 2021 The Noverre Press

CONTENTS

	Page
INTRODUCTION	7
Old Dances of the Isles	8
Highland Dances	9
Strathspeys and Reels	11
Other Country Dances	14
A Royal Visit	15
Music	16
Costume	17
Where Dancing May Be Seen	18
THE DANCES	19
Poise of Body, Arm Positions and Holds	20
Basic Steps	20
Dance Formations	23
Strathspey and Reel	25
Miss Falconer's Fancy	30
The Highland Fling	32
Seann Triubhas	35
BIBLIOGRAPHY	40

Illustrations in Colour, pages 2, 12, 29, 39
Map of Scotland, page 6

INTRODUCTION

SCOTLAND is a country rich in folklore, song, music and dance, and contrary to the general belief this native wealth does not belong exclusively to the Highlands. No solid historical evidence informs us of early dances, but in Court and Castle we may take it that French fashions made themselves felt, and that long before the time of Mary, Queen of Scots. Sources of vivid information are the many ordinances against guising and dancing thundered out by the Protestant reformers who knew neither humanity nor a sense of proportion. At Perth in 1577 eight men 'confest to be of Corpus Christi players' and were made to promise never 'to mell with sik thingis again'. Yet Edinburgh Municipality ventured to organise a Sword dance and a Highland dance for Anne of Denmark in 1590, and twenty-six years later they paid for 'the Hobby horfs and boy fra Berwick', and again for 'tackettes to the hobbie horfs'. At Elgin, in 1623, where the people seemed especially obstinate in their love of old ways, guisers were censured for a Sword dance 'in the Kirk yard'.*

Sword dances of the Hilt-and-Point type, now receded to south of the Border † and to Shetland, seem to have been fairly common in Scotland. A famous one belonged to the Perth Glovers' Corporation. We have records of its performance from 1617 (the Glovers' records only begin in 1593), the most notable being that before Charles I in 1633. That it belonged to the ornate type of Guild Sword

* All the above references are from A. J. Mill, *Medieval Plays in Scotland*, Edinburgh, 1927.
† See *Dances of England and Wales* in this series.

dance the well-known account confirms. 'His Majestie's Chair being set upon the wall next the Tay, whereupon was a flat stage of timber, clad about with birks, upon the which, for his Majestie's welcome and entry, thirteen of our bretheren of this our calling of Glovers, with green caps, strings, red ribbons, white shoes, with bells about their legs, shering rapers in their hands, and all other abulzement, danced our sword dance with many different knots and allafallajessa, five being under and five upon their shoulders, three of them dancing through their feet, drink of wine, and breaking glasses about them, which (God be praised) was acted without hurt or skaith to any . . .'*

Country Sword dances would interest us more, but none remain alive until we come to far Papa Stour, the little Shetland isle. This is a true Hilt-and-Point Sword dance, and the dancers have somehow acquired the name of the Seven Champions of Christendom from the much-travelled St. George and the Dragon stories of Richard Johnson, an Elizabethan hack writer. Their lines are not however those which, from the same source, gave us the Mummers' Play.

OLD DANCES OF THE ISLES

No historical records tell us of dances in the Highlands, but memory still holds them. The following description of the almost forgotten Cailleach an Dudain (Carlin of the Mill Dust) came to me some time since. There was something mysterious about it; news of its performance, whispered about, led to some firelit out-of-the-way house. During general dancing a quarrel sprang up and a man was left 'dead', covered by a white cloth. Laments arose, the local wise woman suddenly appeared, to walk round and round the body muttering an incantation; she then began a dignified dance, withdrawing the cloth and always gazing on the 'dead' face. She touched his hand, his foot, his

* *Statistical Account of Scotland*, vol. x, 1845.

arm, his leg, and all in turn began to shake. She bent to touch his forehead, and up jumped the dead man to dance again while—so great had been the tension—the wise woman was frequently carried out in a faint.

Alexander Carmichael* describes it somewhat differently: the man holding a magic wand, actually then called 'druidic wand', the woman lying 'dead'. Both these descriptions came from Uist. Carmichael tells us too of dances called Combat of the Cocks, Reeling of the Black-cocks, Contest of the Warriors. The Sword dance—meaning the Gillie Callum type—had eight sections instead of four, the Reel of Tulloch eight figures. So our inheritance dwindles away.

There are, however, a number of Step dances in the Islands, especially in South Uist, which are of great interest and are still danced. The Hebridean Weaving Lilt has just been recaptured, and others await collection.

HIGHLAND DANCES

These, the best-known (especially abroad) of all our dances, are often presumed to be our only ones. They are seen wherever there are Scots in the world. In their birthplace they have never died, owing perhaps to the fact that many Highlanders belong to the Roman Catholic Church which, more generous than the new reformers, never attempted to deprive the people of their natural arts and amusements.

These 'step dances', coming to the cities, got into the hands of long-ago dancing masters who polished and stylised till the country and mountain style had completely vanished. Their *raison d'être* today seems to be exhibition; and owing to the rigorous training required for competition and exhibition they have become so standardised that from Tweed to Cape Wrath dancers will give identical performances. I say Tweed advisedly, for they now belong to Highlands and Lowlands alike. Best known amongst them

* *Carmina Gadelica*, vol. I.

is the solo Sword dance, Gillie Callum. The dancer crosses his sword and scabbard, or two swords, on the ground and performs steps over them and in the angles formed by them. Two other Sword dances there are, unfortunately seldom seen; these, the Lochaber and the Argyll Broadswords, are for four men. They begin with swaggering movements, the swords raised horizontally above the dancers' heads, but afterwards laid on the ground, and the stepping over them begins as in Gillie Callum. Just now only the Scottish regiments favour these 'four-handed' Sword dances, but they may come back into fashion. The over-the-crossed-swords type seems to have no relationship to the Hilt-and-Point dance as seen at Perth, Papa Stour and in Northern England. Yet about 1870 in Fife a link appears. Two swords were placed on the ground, two men danced over them, six others ringing them in with swords pointed at them. When all, changing places, had danced inside the pointing swords, the swords on the ground were snatched up. Seven formed a ring round the eighth man, their swords pointing at his throat.* Here appears the ' victim ' of the Hilt-and-Point type.

If this single relic be accepted, it shows at least one important step on the road from ritual to exhibition.

Another warriors' dance is the famous Highland Fling supposed to have been 'stepped' upon a targe, the round metal or hide-covered shield of the mountain man. Because it must be accurately done on so small a spot the intricate stepping is supremely difficult.

Seann Triubhas (The Old Trews) is a dance with a history. It is a man's miming solo dance. Its name was given in derision of the trews thrust perforce upon the Highlanders when, after the rising in support of Prince Charlie in 1745, the kilt, the bagpipes and much else of Highland tradition were forbidden. The trews in the eighteenth century were worn by chiefs and might have been considered an honour-

* Douglas Kennedy, *Proc. Scot. Anthropol. and Folklore Soc.*, 1949.

able article of dress, but the clansmen despised them and various flicks of the fingers and quick turns of the wrists indicate derision and abhorrence of the tight, confining things and longing for the freedom of the kilt. Yet the dance itself must have been a favourite and the teaching of it went on; in 1805, for example, we see a little girl dressed out in yellow shoes performing it in an Edinburgh drawing-room. Alexander Carmichael mentions it, some time previous to 1860, as being danced on Uist and containing much more acting than now.

STRATHSPEYS AND REELS

These eminently Scottish forms of the old Hey or Figure of Eight are now seen in Islands, Highlands and Lowlands alike and have become part of every ballroom programme. How the first became thus called we do not certainly know, but Strath Spey may perhaps have been its birthplace. It is now done in a gliding manner to a moderate, smooth rhythm after which the lively Reel tempo and Reel steps come as an exciting change—for a Reel always follows a Strathspey.

How the ballet step called Pas de Basque—which incidentally is an authentic Basque step used in the Marche des Masquerades by traditional Basque dancers—found a place in the Reel, as in most Scottish dancing, is an intriguing question. The answer seems to be: through French dancing masters. If so, it could only have been through its ballet connection, and that not before the mid-eighteenth century. What, then, was the Reel step previous to its introduction? Is there perhaps a truly traditional Reel step still to be found in unsophisticated places? French dances, fashionable in ballrooms, influenced our native dances as they did in nearly every European country. We read of an Alman Moreis, and as early as the great days of 1745 we find Prince Charles Edward Stuart asking for a 'Strathspey

Plate 2
*Newhaven Fishwives:
working and gala costumes*

Minuet'*—anything more incongruous than this coupling of Country and Court can hardly be imagined. Fashionable London dancing masters too laid down that only those fully trained in the graces of the Minuet could competently perform a Country dance; and a century later we see the same thing happening, the Border Country Dance Valse, for instance, introducing the fashionable Valse step into Country dance figures.

The popular Eightsome Reel should perhaps come under the next heading; but to follow an attempted classification, having looked at Four-handed Reels and learning that Three-handed Reels were an older form, we now examine the Eightsome. This is not more than some eighty years old and was evolved for a ball at the Atholl Gathering while the company was trying to resuscitate a Round Reel, already forgotten. What they did was to give us an exciting combination of figure dance and Reel.

The oldest Reel is probably the Reel of Tulloch. We get glimpses of this from past centuries, once again from the Isle of Uist about 1860, when it had eight figures with 'side issues'. It may be danced at balls by ladies and gentlemen, but when sprung into by four men and the *hooch* rings out as their kilts swirl, their arms strongly linked and, vis-à-vis, they cut and leap, the Reel of Tulloch might then enter into the category of Highland Step dances.

An amusing picture of Reels in an Edinburgh ballroom in the early eighteenth century is given by a Captain Topham, an English visitor to our capital. 'When the company tired of conversation', he writes, 'they began to dance reels. The perseverance which the ladies discover in these reels is not less surprising than their attachment to them. They will sit totally unmoved at the most sprightly airs of an English Country dance, but the moment one of these tunes is played, which is liquid laudanum to my spirits, up they start . . . and you would imagine they had . . . been

* *Scottish Country Dance Society's Bulletin,* March 1936.

bit by a tarantula. . . . Here I have seen four gentlemen perform one of these reels seemingly with the same pleasure . . . as they would have done had they had the most sprightly girl for a partner . . . and they give you the idea that they could with equal glee cast off round a joint stool or set to a cupboard.'

OTHER COUNTRY DANCES

Strathspeys and Reels are accepted as Country dances when used in the ballroom,* but there is another category, figure dances in longways and other forms, more correctly termed Country dances. The longways type, common to the whole of the British Isles, belongs to our Lowlands and Highlands alike. We have a little information about these figure dances from the *Complaynt of Scotland*, 1549, which is concerned with Lowland dances enjoyed by shepherds who 'Quhen this dansing vas dune tha departit . . . to cal there scheip to ther scheip cottis, thai bleu up there bagpipes . . .'. The shepherds danced in a ring; every old shepherd led his wife by the hand, and every young shepherd led her whom he 'luffet' best. They danced to a drone bagpipe, a fiddle and 'ane quhissil', and the names of their dances, some of which probably were Country dances, were Al cristyn mennis dance, The North of Scotland, Huntisup (a Tudor English air which had crossed the Border), Robene Hude, the Alman Haye (interesting in view of the modern figure called Alman and an early reference to the European Allemande dance), The Speyde, The Flail and other intriguing titles.

On both sides of the Border the Country dance grew in favour, went to the great houses and to Court, living on all the time in the countryside and, no doubt, gathering elegance from French and Court fashions. In the early nineteenth century we see Reels and Country dances at

* This seems a modern classification. An older generation did not thus include them.—*The Editor*.

Penny Weddings (where every guest paid a penny towards the entertainment) and learn that in 1801 a Ring dance, which the sixteenth-century shepherds danced, was still a favourite in southern Scotland. In fact we have never ceased to dance Country dances and when, after the First World War, we set about re-introducing them into our social life, collecting and notating them, our material was ready to our hands—a living tradition. They belong and always have belonged to all grades of society. What the Chief or Laird danced the members of the clan danced; therefore our dances are the same in ballrooms and in barns. In the cities they had been forgotten, in the countryside debased by the itinerant teacher who went to villages on a motor-cycle and spread American jazz.

A ROYAL VISIT

The proposed visit of George IV to Edinburgh was not at first acclaimed. Not since Charles II had visited the city in 1650 had a reigning monarch set foot therein; the House of Hanover was disliked, and the city received the news with mixed feelings. Sir Walter Scott valiantly undertook the organisation of the King's reception and decided to make it as Scottish as possible. Highland chiefs brought kilted clansmen, pipers were engaged, 'Edinburgh went tartan-mad'. Highland dress and bagpipes had been tentatively rising from their banishment. Now every Edinburgh gentleman produced a kilt. The King threw himself into the spirit of the reception and, landing at Leith with a thistle in his Admiral's hat, announced that he too would wear the kilt at his levee. To the remark that trews would be more seemly on so stout a king, Lady Saltoun retorted that 'since his stay was so short the more we see of him the better'. When the great appearance was made, flesh-coloured tights could be descried below the kilt; but General Stewart of Garth, who supervised the robing, was pleased to see in the result 'a verra pretty man'.* From that moment Scottish customs and traditions, including tartans, games, dancing and pipe-playing, came into their own again.

MUSIC

Gaelic songs and music differ from those of the Lowlands in rhythm—owing to the language—in the use of the ancient gapped scales, and above all in an archaic emotional content. They are now the detritus of an older society, already half forgotten when Alexander Carmichael wrote down the words—alas, not the music. Much work has been and is being done in the collection of what remains of this strange, antique treasure.

Lowland songs in the Scottish dialect of the English language suffered a calamity when, after the famous visit of George IV, everything Scottish became the fashion. Poetical ladies wrote verses in 'National' style—but in this they only copied Robert Burns—to old or new tunes, and these were so well received that they have actually taken the place of traditional folk songs. A few lovely traditional Lowland songs are now being collected, and something of the discarded traditional words can be found in T. F. Henderson's *Scottish Vernacular Literature*.

The small Celtic harp, the clarsach, is now being revived and charming it is to see, set on its stool, and charming to hear, though faint in tone, when accompanying a Gaelic song. Clarsach ensembles are untraditional.

Dance music is sometimes provided by the human voice. *Puirt a beul* or mouth music must enunciate words, so for dancing it is gay, but breathless.

Bagpipes belong to the whole of Scotland. In the south the small pipes, akin to those of Northumbria, were used but the great pipes superseded them. The great pipes pro-

* Much of this description is from Janet Adam Smith, *Radio Times*, June 25th, 1937.

duce the pentatonic scale, the bag measures about 2 ft. 2 in. long, the bass drone about 3 ft. This is a very moderate size compared with the whole pigskins of the Italian Abruzzi and Calabria round which the player's arms will barely reach. Heartrending laments, called in Gaelic *piobaireachd* (anglicised to pibroch), are considered the highest form of pipe-music; Reels and Strathspeys are inspiring for dancing.

When after the '45 the pipes were forbidden Chiefs replaced their pipers by fiddlers—yet Robertson, 'pipe maker, Castle Hill', was making them in 1775, and in 1781 Scotsmen in London founded a Highland society for pipe competitions in the very capital of the Hanoverian King.

A famous fiddler was Niel Gow, who composed and collected hundreds of dance tunes now forming a wonderful national treasure. Fiddlers are still popular for dancing, pipes more so, while all over Scotland orchestras specialising in Scottish dance music are being formed. These are particularly suitable to ballrooms.

COSTUME

Since 1822 Highland costume has had a period of development. Tartans are made for every clan; the kilt is seen in Edinburgh as in the north. As an evening dress for men it is most becoming and fashionable; for general country wear it grows more and more popular and many boys never wear trousers until they reach manhood. Evening doublets are of saxe blue, wine colour or green, to which the lace jabots give a finishing elegance. Plaids are used as cloaks in the mountains; with the kilt the Balmoral or Glengarry bonnet is correct. In a ballroom ladies wear light or white evening dresses, their clan tartan appearing in a sash passed over the left shoulder (Plate 3). In the daytime a tartan skirt is popular—the kilt is for the man, not for the woman. If a man has no clan tartan he may wear a kilt of grey or of a regional tartan.

In the remote countryside the shortgown and petticoat, which was the dress of the countrywoman until recently, may still be seen as shown in Plate 1.

The Newhaven (on the Firth of Forth) fishwife in her traditional costume still sells fish from the creel on her back as did her ancestress centuries ago. She possesses a gala costume as well as her working dress (Plate 2).

The tartan trews, once the prerogative of the Chieftain or Laird, are hardly seen today except in the uniform of certain Scottish regiments.

OCCASIONS WHEN DANCING MAY BE SEEN

Highland games or gatherings are held all over Scotland in the summer. The best-known are at Braemar, Dunoon (Cowal Games), Oban, Aboyne and Inverness.

Highland sports, such as Tossing the Caber, are to be seen at the gatherings, as well as bagpipe competitions, and many classes of dancing competitions.

Dancing may also be seen at pipe band meetings. Dates must be ascertained locally.

For many years past, girls have flooded the dance competitions, performing men's dances in a travesty of men's dress. There is now, however, a growing feeling against this, and although a large section of Scots accept what is a degradation of a fine male tradition, there are signs of an awakening. At the Braemar and Aboyne gatherings girls, though still permitted to compete, must appear in a white blouse and tartan skirt.

The Scottish Country Dance Society, Thornhill, Cairnmuir Road, Edinburgh 12, will give information as to Country dancing in Edinburgh or at any of its branches.

THE DANCES

TECHNICAL EDITORS
MURIEL WEBSTER AND KATHLEEN P. TUCK

ABBREVIATIONS
USED IN DESCRIPTION OF DANCES AND STEPS

r—right ⎱ referring to
l—left ⎰ hand, foot, etc.

R—right ⎱ describing turns or
L—left ⎰ ground pattern

C—clockwise

C-C—counter-clockwise

For descriptions of foot positions and explanations of any ballet terms the following books are suggested for reference:

A Primer of Classical Ballet (Cecchetti method). Cyril Beaumont.

First Steps (R.A.D.). Ruth French and Felix Demery.

The Ballet Lover's Pocket Book. Kay Ambrose.

Reference books for description of figures:

The Scottish Country Dance Society's Publications. Many volumes, from Thornhill, Cairnmuir Road, Edinburgh 12.

The English Folk Dance and Song Society's Publications. Cecil Sharp House, 2 Regent's Park Road, London, N.W.1.

The Country Dance Book I–VI. Cecil J. Sharp. Novello & Co., London.

POISE OF BODY, ARM POSITIONS AND HOLDS

In all Scottish dancing—Country dancing and Highland—the body is held erect, with the head well poised.

Scottish Country (Ballroom) Dancing. The women always hold their skirts; the men's arms hang to sides. The man leads the woman by the right hand (unless otherwise indicated), and may turn her with one hand if the Skip-change-of-step is danced, or with both hands when dancing the Pas de Basque.

Highland Dancing. There are two positions of arms which are characteristic of Highland Dancing.

1. Hands on waist. Wrists flat with the back of the wrists facing forward, knuckles placed on the waist.

2. Arms raised. (*a*) Both arms curved in front of the head, palms facing one another, about eighteen inches between, with the thumb touching the first two fingers.

(*b*) One arm raised as above, the other hand on the hip. The general rule is that the opposite arm is raised to the leg that is pointing.

When turning partners the men link first r then l arms, the free arm being raised above the head.

Other Arm Movements are described in the Seann Triubhas.

BASIC STEPS

The Country-dance steps are less elaborate than the Highland but all steps may be classified as either (*a*) Jig or Reel Steps or (*b*) Strathspey Steps.

REEL STEPS: SCOTTISH COUNTRY DANCING

	MUSIC Beats
Skip-Change-of-Step. A travelling step forward or backward. (*N.B.* Count '4 1 2 3' in Reel time instead of 'and 1 and 2' in Jig time as here described.)	
Hop on l foot, lifting r leg forward, knee and ankle extended and leg turned out (foot a few inches from ground);	and
step forward on r foot;	1
close l foot to r foot in 3rd position behind;	and
step forward on r foot.	2
Repeat, hopping on r foot.	
Pas de Basque. A setting or turning step.	
'Set once' means 2 Pas de Basque.	
Spring from l foot, making a very small and quick circular movement to R with r foot, knee and ankle extended, before landing on r foot;	and 1
close l foot in 3rd position in front, changing weight;	and
change weight to r foot in 3rd position behind, extending l foot outward.	2
Repeat, springing on to l foot.	

REEL STEPS: HIGHLAND DANCING (3 EXAMPLES)

Chassé. Similar to the Skip-change-of-step used in Country Dancing.

Pas de Basque and Change

One Pas de Basque on to r foot as in Country dancing, using 5th position instead of 3rd;	1 and 2
spring r foot in front of l foot in 5th position, weight on balls of both feet;	1
spring l foot in front of r foot in 5th position, weight on balls of both feet.	2
Repeat whole step on to l foot.	

Toe and Off. Travelling step to L, then R.

Hop on l foot, placing r toe in 5th position in front;	1
hop on l foot, extending r leg to raised 2nd position (shake);	2
glide r foot behind l foot in 5th position;	1
step sideways on l foot, travelling to L;	and
glide r foot behind l foot, cutting l foot to raised 2nd position.	2

Repeat with l foot, hopping on r foot.

STRATHSPEY STEPS: SCOTTISH COUNTRY DANCING

Travelling Strathspey Step

Glide r foot forward, 'giving' in l knee and ankle before stepping forward on r foot;	1
close l foot to r foot in 3rd position behind;	2
step forward on r foot;	3
hop on r foot, bringing l foot through close to ground, knee turned out and ankle extended.	4

Repeat on l foot.

Common Schottische. Setting step.

Step to R on r foot;	1
close l foot to 3rd position behind;	2
step to R on r foot ;	3
hop on r foot, placing l foot behind r ankle, knee turned out and ankle extended.	4

Repeat to L on l foot.

STRATHSPEY STEPS: HIGHLAND DANCING

Travelling Strathspey. This step is similar to that described above under Scottish Country, but the dancer is higher on the toes, and on the 4th beat the l foot is placed on the shin of the r leg while hopping on the r foot.

Highland Schottische
  Hop on l foot, pointing r foot to 2nd position; | 1
  hop on l foot, placing r foot behind the calf of l leg; | 2
  hop on l foot, pointing r foot to 2nd or 4th position; | 3
  hop on l foot, placing r foot against l shin; | 4
  one Common Schottische step to R. | 1 2 3 4
  Repeat, hopping on r foot.

Double Toe-off
  Hop on l foot, beating r toe lightly to 5th position in front; | 1
  hop on l foot, extending r leg to raised 2nd position; | 2
  repeat beats 1 and 2; | 3 4
  glide r foot behind l heel; | 1
  step to L on l foot; | 2
  glide r foot behind l heel; | 3
  hop on r foot, extending l foot to raised 2nd position. | 4
  Repeat on opposite foot.

༻༺

DANCE FORMATIONS

The Scottish Country Dance has a great variety of formations, only two of which are described here.

THE ALLEMANDE (see Plate 3). This is a method of progression whereby the 1st couple and 2nd couple change places.

The Grasp or Hold. 1st couple stand in the middle of the set, facing the top. The man lifts his partner's r hand in his r hand over and behind her head, joining l hand in front to lead her. The 2nd couple stand immediately behind the 1st couple with the same grasp.

The whole progression takes 8 bars of music and may be danced to (*a*) Reel or Jig time—8 Skip-change-of-steps; (*b*) Strathspey time—8 travelling Strathspey steps, thus:—

1. 1st couple move diagonally forward to R;
2. wheel on the spot to face the men's side;
3. move to men's side of the set;
4. a long step down the dance on men's side;
5. move slightly toward centre turning side by side (woman on man's R) to face women's side of set;
6. man swings woman under her own arm to face him, both hands crossed, moving to centre of set;
7. } partners move back to own side of dance, one place
8. } down, with two short steps.

The 2nd couple follow close behind the 1st couple for the first three steps and finish above them on the fourth step. They dance the next four steps as described and finish in 1st couple's place. The whole movement is danced within the set.

RIGHTS AND LEFTS. May be danced to a Reel, Jig or Strathspey tune. Partners change places, giving r hands; change places with side partners, giving l hands. This is called 'Half Rights and Lefts' and is often used as a method of progression, as the two couples have now changed places. To complete the figure, dancers complete the square by changing places with own partner (r hands) and side partner (l hands).

The whole figure usually takes 8 bars of music, in which case two steps are taken to each handing.

On the last change with l hands, dancers turn toward their side partner to face the centre of the set.

STRATHSPEY AND REEL (*Foursome Reel*)

Region Widespread.

Character The Ballroom version is simple and dignified. The Highland version has more elaborate steps.

Formation A dance for 2 couples consisting of an alternate 'Cutting the figure of eight' and setting to partner. (○ = woman, □ = man.)

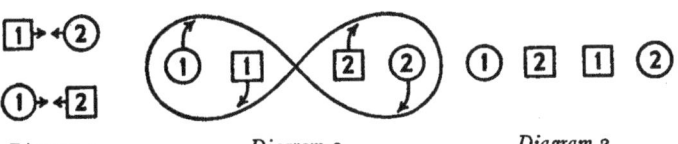

Diagram 1   *Diagram 2*   *Diagram 3*

Dance. Part I: Strathspey-time

BOW AND CURTSEY

The dancers stand side by side as in Diagram 1 and bow or curtsey to own partner.

MUSIC
Bars
a chord

The two men then step forward and turn to R to face own partners, so that they are back to back with one another.

a chord

STEP I: CUTTING THE FIGURE

All dance 8 Strathspey travelling steps, making the pattern of a figure of eight (see Diagram 2).

Dancers pass own partners and opposite partner by r shoulders on the outside and own sex by l shoulders in centre. The two

Strathspey
A
1–4
repeated

STRATHSPEY: Miss Drummond of Perth

Arranged by Arnold Foster

Follow with Reel *tune*

REEL : Loch Earn

Arranged by Arnold Foster

Play Strathspey, *then* Reel *twice through with repeats*

men turn in, to face opposite lady on the last step instead of passing l shoulders with one another (Diagram 3).

STEP II: SET TO PARTNERS
All set to opposite partner with any Strathspey step.

B
5–12

STEP III: CUTTING THE FIGURE
Repeat the Cutting of the Figure, to finish facing own partner.

A
1–4
repeated

STEP IV: SET TO PARTNER
As in Step II.

B
5–12

Part II: Reel-time
Steps I, II, III and IV are now repeated in reel time.
To cut the figure (Steps I & III) 8 Skip-change-of-steps (Chassés) are used. To set to opposite partner and own partner (Steps II & IV) any Reel Steps may be used. Each step takes 8 bars of music. The number of times that the figure is cut may vary, but dancers must always finish facing own partners.

Reel-tune twice through with repeats

Plate 3   The Allemande figure in 'Miss Falconer's Fancy'

MISS FALCONER'S FANCY

Region   Little known—collected about 1800.

Character   A Scottish Country dance in reel-time, showing a variety of formations.

Formation   Longwise set for four couples. Partners face one another about two or three yards apart, men with l shoulders towards the top of the set. Couples stand at arm's length from one another and are numbered in threes.

Dance	MUSIC
Bow and Curtsey—men hands to sides, ladies hold skirts.	*Bars* a chord
STEP I: SET AND CAST	A
1st couple set to each other with 2 Pas de Basque and cast off one place on own side of the dance with 2 Skip-change-of-steps.	1–4
Repeat the setting and cast up to own places.	5–8
STEP II: DOWN THE MIDDLE AND UP AGAIN	B
1st couple lead down the middle with 3 Skip-change-of-steps, turning on the 4th step; dance up the middle cast round the 2nd couple on own side of the dance and lead up to the top of the set. (8 Skip-change-of-steps for the whole figure.)	9–16
STEP III: ALLEMANDE (see 'Dance Formations')	A
1st and 2nd couples dance the Allemande with 8 Skip-change-of-steps.	1–8
STEP IV: HANDS FOUR ROUND AND BACK	B
1st and 3rd couples join hands in a ring and slip 8 steps to L and 8 steps back to R.	9–16

MISS FALCONER'S FANCY

Tune: *Miss Forbes' Farewell to Banff*

Play A, B, A, B B as often as desired

STEP V: RIGHTS AND LEFTS (see 'Dance Formations')   B 9–16

1st and 2nd couples dance Rights and Lefts, taking 2 Skip-change-of-steps to each handing.

Repeat, having progressed one place.

THE HIGHLAND FLING

Region   Highlands originally, but now widespread.

Character   A lively and virile dance requiring great agility and precision of footwork.

Formation   A solo dance for men.

Dance	MUSIC
This dance has a great variety of steps, which may be performed in any order. Only four steps are described.	*Bars*
THE BOW. Feet in first position, hands down by the sides, incline head and shoulders slightly forward and rise upright with no exaggeration. Hands are then placed on waist.	a chord
	A
STEP I: ROUND THE LEG	1
Spring and point r foot in 2nd position;	(beat 1)
hop on l foot, placing r foot behind the calf of l leg;	(beat 2)
hop on l foot, placing r foot in front of l shin, heel just below knee;	(beat 3)
hop on l foot, placing r foot behind the calf as in beat 2.	(beat 4)
(The movements of beats 2, 3, 4 are called 'Round the Leg' and will be so described.)	
Spring and point l foot in 2nd position and dance Round the Leg with l foot.	2
Repeat the movements described in bar 1.	3
Repeat the movements described in bar 2, turning to R after pointing the l foot in 2nd position.	4

MARQUIS OF HUNTLY'S HIGHLAND FLING

Play twice through with repeats

Repeat the whole series, beginning with l foot and turning to R.	1-4
Arms. The opposite arm up to moving leg, the other hand on hip, *i.e.* Arms in Opposition.	
	B
STEP II: HIGHLAND SCHOTTISCHE	5
Spring and point r foot in 2nd position;	(beat 1)
hop on l foot, placing r foot behind the calf of l leg;	(beat 2)
hop on l foot, pointing r foot either in 2nd or 4th position;	(beat 3)

hop on l foot, placing r foot in front of l shin.	(beat 4)
Repeat above, beginning with l foot.	6
Repeat above, beginning with r foot.	7
Turn to the R as in 4th bar of Step I (Round the Leg).	8
Repeat the whole movement, beginning with l foot and turning to L.	5–8

STEP III: TOE AND HEEL — A

Repeat the movements of Step I, bar 1 (Round the Leg).	1
Spring on r foot, placing l toe in 5th position in front;	2 / (beat 1)
hop on r foot, placing l heel in 5th position in front;	(beat 2)
repeat the toe-heel movements with r foot, hopping on l foot;	(beats 3, 4)
repeat the toe-heel movements with l foot, then with r foot;	3
turn to R, as in 4th bar of Step I.	4
Repeat the whole movement, beginning with l foot and turning to L.	1–4
Hands on waist for Toe and Heel movements (bars 2 and 3).	

STEP IV: ROUND THE LEG (DOUBLE TURN) — B

Repeat Step I, bar 1, three times with r foot;	5–7
turn to R with same movement with l foot.	8
Repeat Step I, bar 2, twice with l foot;	5–6
turn twice to L with Round the Leg twice with r foot pointing r foot in 2nd position before each turn. Arms in opposition throughout.	7–8
The dance finishes with another Bow.	a chord

SEANN TRIUBHAS (*The Old Trews*)

Region Highlands originally, now widespread.

Character Slow and flowing, with graceful yet virile movement.

Formation A solo dance for men. See Plate 4.

Dance	MUSIC
This dance consists of a Slow Part, usually four Steps, and a Quick Part, two Steps.	Bars
THE BOW. As in the Highland Fling, but the arms are raised above the head and r foot placed forward in 4th position after the Bow.	a chord
The Slow Part. STEP I: THE CIRCLE	A
Hop on l foot, bending and stretching r knee forward to raised 4th position;	1 (beat 1)
repeat the above movement;	(beat 2)
spring on r foot and repeat beats 1 and 2 kicking l leg lightly forward;	(beats 3, 4)
repeat on l, r, l, r feet—i.e. two hops on each foot.	2–3
The movement is a travelling one, the dancer moving C-C in a small circle to finish facing forward for the Shuffle step.	
4 Shuffles on l, r, l, r feet.	4
Repeat the circle, travelling C and starting on r foot.	1–3
4 Shuffles on r, l, r, l feet.	4
Arms are raised during the circle and held on waist for Shuffles.	

STEP II: SIDE STEP	B
Hop on l foot, bending and stretching r knee to 'shake' r foot sideways into 2nd position, about 1 foot off the floor;	5 (beat 1)
close r foot behind l foot in 5th position;	(beat 2)
glide l foot gently to L;	(and)
close r foot behind l foot in 5th position;	(beat 3)
glide l foot to L; close r foot behind l foot in 5th position.	(and 4)
Repeat the movement, 'shaking' l foot sideways and travelling to R.	6
Repeat the movement, 'shaking' the r leg sideways and travelling to L.	7
4 Shuffles on l, r, l, r feet.	8
Repeat the whole movement, hopping on r foot and finishing with 4 Shuffles on r, l, r, l feet.	5–8
Arms. On the 1st beat of the side-step, i.e. 'Shake', the arms are raised quickly forward upward, and head is turned slightly to R.	
On beats 2 and 3 and 4 the arms are slowly opened and lowered sideways downward. Hands on waist for Shuffles.	
STEP III: BRUSH STEP	A
Hop on l foot with r foot slightly extended and bend r knee so that the r toe is brushed lightly along the floor towards l toe;	1 (and 1)
beat r toe in 5th position ('and'); stamp l foot in 5th position behind;	(and 2)
hop twice on l foot shaking r leg twice in raised 2nd position;	(3 and)
spring r foot under l heel extending l foot forward (coupé).	(beat 4)
Repeat, beginning with hop on r foot.	2

SEANN TRIUBHAS

Arranged by Arnold Foster

Play twice through with repeats, then follow with the Marquis of Huntly once through (with repeats) at a quicker tempo.

Repeat the first 2 beats of Bar 1;	3 (& 1 & 2)
spring on r foot, extending l foot forward in raised 4th position;	(beat 3)
spring on l foot, extending r foot forward in raised 4th position.	(beat 4)

Repeat the first 2 beats of Bar 1 with r foot;	4 (beats 1, 2)
extend r foot forward, then quickly place r foot in front of l leg, behind l heel, and turn quickly on balls of both feet to L— one whole turn.	(beats 3, 4)
Repeat the whole movement, hopping on r foot and finishing with turn to R about.	1–4

Arms in opposition except on the 2 Springs (Bar 3, beats 3, 4), when both arms are raised, and on the Turns (Bar 4, beats 3, 4), when hands are on waist.

STEP IV: COUPÉ	B
Hop on l foot, beating r foot against l shin and extending it to raised 4th position;	5 (beat 1)
glide r foot forward; close l foot behind r in 5th position.	(and 2)
Spring on r foot, leaving l leg extended backward (Coupé over);	(beat 3)
beat l foot against r shin and extend l leg forward, hopping on r foot;	(and 4)
Coupé over on to l foot; step back on r foot; close l foot 5th in front.	6 (b'ts 1 & 2)
Coupé under on r foot; step forward on l foot; close r 5th behind.	(b'ts 3 & 4)
Repeat bars 5 and 6, beginning with hop on r foot.	7–8
Repeat the whole movement, hopping on l and r feet.	5–8

Arms. Described under music bars:—
Bar 5: (beats 1, 2) Arms in opposition; (beats 3, 4) both arms up.
Bar 6: (beats 1, 2) both arms lowered slowly sideways downward on to waist;

Plate 4
Seann Triubhas
and great pipes

(beats 3, 4) both arms raised sideways upward.

Quick Part — Highland Fling
At the end of the last step, the dancer claps his hands to indicate the change of time. He then dances any two Steps of the Highland Fling.

16 bars quicker tempo

BIBLIOGRAPHY

CARMICHAËL, ALEXANDER.—*Carmina Gadelica*, vol. I. 2nd ed. 1928, Edinburgh and London.
COLLIE, GEORGE F.—*Highland Dress*. Penguin Books, London, 1948.
FLOOD, WM. H. GRATTAN.—*The Story of the Bagpipe*. London, 1911.
JOHNSON, ALEXANDER.—*The Sword Dance of Papa Stour, Shetland*. Lerwick, 1926.
KAY, J. MEREDITH.—*The Gleneagles Collection of Old Scottish Dance Tunes*. Edinburgh, 1924.
KENNEDY, DOUGLAS, in the *Proceedings of the Scottish Anthropological and Folklore Society*, vol. IV, No. 1, 1949. Edinburgh.
LEYDEN, JOHN.—Preface to the 1801 edition of *The Complaynt of Scotland*.
MACDONALD, KEITH NORMAN.—*Puirt-a-Beul. Mouth Music*. (Gaelic words. Tunes in Sol-fa.) Oban Times, 1901.
MACKENZIE, D. R.—*The National Dances of Scotland: Eightsomes, Foursomes, Flings and some other Scottish Dances*. Glasgow, 1940.
MILL, A. J.—*Medieval Plays in Scotland*. Edinburgh, 1927.
SCOTTISH COUNTRY DANCE SOCIETY.—Scottish Country Dance Books. Many volumes. Edinburgh.
WOOD, MELUSINE.—'Some Notes on Trade Tools and Ritual Dance. *Journal of the English Folk Dance and Song Society*, vol. IV, no. 6, 1945.

There are numberless collections of Strathspey and Reel tunes. Niel Gow and his sons published many collections of fiddle tunes in the early nineteenth century.

www.ingramcontent.com/pod-product-compliance
Lightning Source LLC
Chambersburg PA
CBHW061743290426
43661CB00127B/970